Up on the Housetop

Illustrated by Andrea Gabriel

Revised by: **Kim Mitzo Thompson, Karen Mitzo Hilderbrand**
Illustrated By: **Andrea Gabriel** Book Design: **Jennifer Birchler**
Publisher: **Twin Sisters Productions, LLC** Song: **Public Domain**
Executive Producers: **Kim Mitzo Thompson, Karen Mitzo Hilderbrand**
Music Arranged By: **Hal Wright** Music Vocals: **The Nashville Kids Sound**

Up on the housetop reindeer pause,

out jumps good old **Santa Claus**.

Down through the chimney with lots of toys,

all for the little ones, **Christmas** joys!

Ho! Ho! Ho! Who wouldn't go?

Ho! Ho! Ho! Who wouldn't go?

Up on the housetop, click, click, click,

down through the chimney with

good **Saint Nick**!

First comes the stocking of little **Nell**.

Oh, dear **Santa** fill it well.

Give her a dolly that laughs and cries,

one that can open and shut its eyes!

Ho! Ho! Ho! Who wouldn't go?

Ho! Ho! Ho! Who wouldn't go?

Up on the housetop, click, click, click,

down through the chimney with

good **Saint Nick**!

Look in the stocking of little **Will**.

Oh, just see what a glorious fill!

Here is a hammer with lots of tacks,

whistle and **ball** and a whip that cracks!

Ho! Ho! Ho! Who wouldn't go?

Ho! Ho! Ho! Who wouldn't go?

Up on the housetop, click, click, click,

down through the chimney with

good **Saint Nick**!

Up on the Housetop

Up on the house - top,—— rein - deer pause, out jumps good old San - ta Claus.
First comes the stock - ing of lit - tle Nell. Oh, dear San - ta fill it well.

Down through the chim - ney with lots of toys, all for the lit - tle ones—— Christ - mas joys!
Give her a dol - ly that laughs and cries, one that can o - pen and shut its eyes.

Ho! Ho! Ho! Who would - n't go? Ho! Ho! Ho! Who would - n't go?——

Up on the house top, click, click, click, down through the chim - ney with good Saint Nick!

Look in the stock - ing of lit - tle Will.

Help Santa find your house on Christmas Eve.

Start

Finish